DEION SANDERS

DEION SANDERS

From Multisport Superstar to Coach Prime

Matt Doeden

LERNER PUBLICATIONS ◆ MINNEAPOLIS

Lerner Publications Company
An imprint of Lerner Publishing Group, Inc.
241 First Avenue North
Minneapolis, MN 55401 USA

For reading levels and more information, look up this title at www.lernerbooks.com.

Main body text set in Rotis Serif Std 55 Regular. Typeface provided by Adobe Systems.

Editor: Nicole Berglund **Designer:** Lauren Cooper **Photo Editor:** Nicole Berglund
Lerner team: Sue Marquis

Library of Congress Cataloging-in-Publication Data

Names: Doeden, Matt author.
Title: Deion Sanders : from multisport superstar to Coach Prime / Matt Doeden.
Description: Minneapolis, MN : Lerner Publications, [2025] | Series: Gateway biographies |
    Includes bibliographical references and index. | Audience: Ages 9–14 | Audience: Grades 4–6
    | Summary: "Deion Sanders starred in both Major League Baseball and the National Football
    League. In 2023 he took the college football world by storm as the coach of the Colorado
    Buffaloes. Explore his life and career"– Provided by publisher.
Identifiers: LCCN 2023057492 (print) | LCCN 2023057493 (ebook) | ISBN 9798765644256
    (library binding) | ISBN 9798765644300 (paperback) | ISBN 9798765644270 (epub)
Subjects: LCSH: Sanders, Deion–Juvenile literature. | Football players–United States–
    Biography–Juvenile literature. | Football coaches–United States–Biography–Juvenile
    literature.
Classification: LCC GV939.S186 D64 2025 (print) | LCC GV939.S186 (ebook) | DDC 796.332092
    [B]–dc23/eng/20231214

LC record available at https://lccn.loc.gov/2023057492
LC ebook record available at https://lccn.loc.gov/2023057493

Manufactured in the United States of America
1-1010109-52451-2/29/2024

TABLE OF CONTENTS

Deion Sanders coaches from the sidelines during a September 2023 game.

The eyes of the college football world were fixed on Deion Sanders as the University of Colorado Buffaloes took the field on September 2, 2023. It was Sanders's first game as head coach of the Buffaloes, and no one knew what to expect.

Sanders was no ordinary coach. Some said he lacked the experience needed to be a major college head coach, while others said he was too brash and bold for the job. He'd forced many players out of Colorado's football program so he could bring in players that he thought would perform better, including two of his sons. However, Sanders's big personality was also a strength. Players responded to him because he was a former National Football League (NFL) star. Coach Prime, as his players called him, had always talked a big game. It was time to see if he could deliver on his promises.

Amon G. Carter Stadium in Fort Worth, Texas, was packed with screaming Texas Christian University (TCU) fans. A year before, TCU had made it all the way to the College Football Playoff National Championship. They were heavily favored to beat Colorado and its unproven head coach.

Sanders patrolled the sidelines in a white Colorado sweatshirt as the teams traded points. Quarterback Shedeur Sanders, Coach Prime's son, led the Buffaloes up and down the field. It was a back-and-forth shootout. Both teams seemed to score at will. The TCU Horned Frogs took the lead, 42–38, with seven minutes remaining

Sanders and son Shedeur talk before the game on September 2, 2023.

in the game. But Shedeur Sanders answered quickly. He threw a 46-yard touchdown to Dylan Edwards to put Colorado back on top.

This time, the Colorado defense held up. TCU's final drive stalled, and the Buffaloes won the game 45–42. Coach Prime and his players rushed onto the field as shocked TCU fans looked on. At least for one week, Deion Sanders had silenced his critics.

During his time as a football player, Sanders had been his own biggest promoter. He loved to tell people how good he was—and he was usually right. Coach Prime was no different. He wanted everyone to know that he had arrived.

"We're gonna continuously be questioned because we do things that have never been done," he said. "And that makes people uncomfortable. When you see a confident Black man sitting up here and talking his talk, walking his walk . . . that's kind of threatening. Oh, they don't like that. But guess what, we're gonna consistently do what we do because I'm here and I ain't going nowhere."

TOUGH START

Deion Luwynn Sanders was born on August 9, 1967, in Fort Myers, Florida. The future star had a rocky start. He lived with his parents, Connie and Mims Sanders, in a rough neighborhood. Deion's father struggled with drug abuse. The couple divorced when Deion was only two

Fort Myers, Florida

years old. "[My father] wasn't there with me," Deion said. "But he was around the corner."

Connie worked several jobs to support Deion. When he was seven, she was working at a hospital. She couldn't be home in the mornings when he got ready for school. So before she left, she would make breakfast and set out clothes for him. Then she'd call him from work to wake him up. He relied on himself to get dressed, eat, and get to school on time.

When Deion was young, Connie married Willie Knight, who became Deion's stepfather. The couple had a daughter, Tracie, who is nine years younger than Deion. Deion's home life was strong, but the family struggled with money. They lived in a small house in a neighborhood with lots of crime. Deion promised his mother that when he grew up, he'd buy her a big, new house.

Deion was always a good athlete, and his talent helped him excel. By the time he reached North Fort Myers High School, it was clear that sports could be his ticket to a better life. He was named an all-state performer in baseball, basketball, and football, which meant he was among the best in the state at all three sports. During one high school basketball game, Deion was especially hot. One of his friends started calling him Prime Time. Even then, Deion was a big talker. He loved to showboat and let people know just how good

Sanders attends an event at North Fort Myers High School in 2015.

he was. The nickname appealed to his big personality, so he ran with it.

Deion wanted to look his best, on and off the court. His style was a big part of who he was, and it reflected his confidence and natural talent as an athlete. But Deion knew that natural talent wasn't enough. If he wanted to be a professional athlete, he would have to put in the work.

People were taking notice. College football programs around the country recruited him to play for their schools. Pro baseball scouts watched his games. Deion had options. The Kansas City Royals chose him in the sixth round of the 1985 Major League Baseball (MLB) draft. He could have signed a contract to make his dream come true straight out of high school. But football remained his passion, and college football was the next step on that career path. In the fall of 1985, he enrolled at Florida State University (FSU) in Tallahassee. He was about to take his talents onto a national stage.

SEMINOLE YEARS

It didn't take long for Sanders to make an impact with the Florida State Seminoles. His sixth game as a freshman was unforgettable. Sanders started with a pair of big punt returns to set up FSU scores. Late in the game, Tulsa drove deep into FSU territory. Quarterback Steve Gage took the snap from the 4-yard line. Gage tossed a quick

Sanders poses with his Jim Thorpe Award at Florida State in 1988.

pass to the left. But Sanders was ready. He darted in front of the receiver to intercept the ball. Then Sanders sidestepped a tackler and streaked all the way down the field for a touchdown.

The big play was a taste of things to come. Sanders quickly became one of the best cornerbacks in the nation. His speed and agility allowed him to stay close to any opposing receiver. And his ability to read the quarterback, paired with his quick hands, made him an interception machine. Legendary FSU head coach Bobby Bowden later called Sanders "the best athlete I ever coached."

But Sanders wasn't only a football player. He also played outfield for FSU baseball and ran track. He was a good hitter, batting .331 as a freshman. The speed that made him good on the track also helped him become a skilled base stealer.

In the summer of 1988, the New York Yankees chose Sanders in the 30th round of the MLB draft. It was the second time he'd been drafted by a professional baseball team, and this time he decided to sign a contract. Sanders played in 28 minor league games for the Yankees that summer. He batted a respectable .284 and showed flashes of the talent that had pro teams so interested. But he also knew that his baseball skills were not as polished as his football skills.

Sanders dives for the ball during a game with the New York Yankees.

"I have a lot to learn, and I know it," he said. "I haven't decided whether to play [professional] baseball or football. All I'm doing is getting ready to play. I'm trying to learn as much as I can about baseball."

As fall approached, Sanders set down his baseball glove and put on his football pads for his final season at FSU. He was better than ever. When Sanders wasn't shutting down opposing receivers, he was leading the nation in punt return average. He won the Jim Thorpe Award as the nation's best defensive back, and he had NFL scouts drooling over his potential.

Doing it All

On May 16, 1987, FSU's baseball and track teams were both playing for conference championships in Columbia, South Carolina. Sanders helped the baseball team win their semifinal game, ran a 4x100 relay for the track team, and then returned to the baseball diamond for the championship game—which FSU won.

His final college game was the 1989 Sugar Bowl. FSU was clinging to a 13–7 lead over Auburn University late in the game. Auburn had the ball at the FSU 22-yard line with just 12 seconds to play. Quarterback Reggie Slack fired a pass toward the end zone. But Sanders jumped the route. He made the interception to seal the victory for FSU. It was a fitting way to end his brilliant college career.

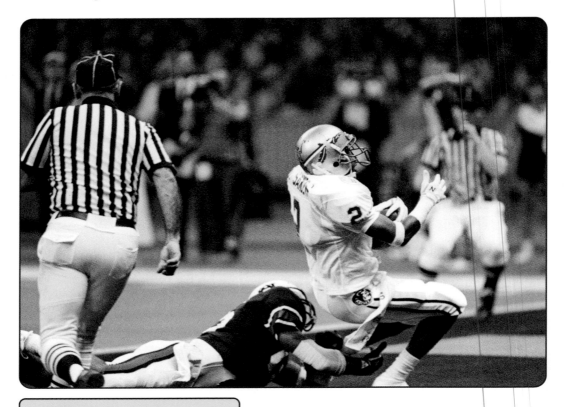

Sanders (*right*) intercepts a pass during the 1989 Sugar Bowl.

TWO-SPORT STAR

The 1989 NFL draft was loaded with talented players. Sanders was one of them. Before the draft, teams interviewed him. The New York Giants had a pick in the middle of the first round, but Sanders wasn't interested when they wanted to talk to him. "I'll be gone before [your pick]," he said as he walked out the door. "I'll see you later."

Sanders wanted to play for the Atlanta Falcons. But players don't get to choose their teams in the draft. Any team that picks them owns their rights. Sanders's baseball career gave him leverage, however. He told other teams that if they drafted him, he'd play baseball instead. They'd end up getting nothing in return for a valuable draft pick. Sanders's tactic worked. The Falcons chose him with the fifth pick. He was headed to Atlanta.

Sanders reacts to being chosen by the Atlanta Falcons in the 1989 NFL draft.

Sanders returned to the Yankees in the summer of 1989. He made his MLB debut on May 31, and it was a memorable one. In the first inning, he threw out a baserunner. Later, he drove in a run and scored a run, helping New York to a 9–5 victory over the Seattle Mariners. Sanders played 14 games for the Yankees that year. He batted only .234, but hit two home runs. It was enough to show that he belonged in the big leagues, even with an NFL career on the horizon.

Sanders bats for the Yankees in 1989.

When the NFL season began, Sanders was ready. In his first game, he fielded a punt and started a return. He broke two tackles then blazed down the field. Nobody could catch him, and he scored a touchdown. The Falcons went on to lose the game, but Sanders gave the team's fans a glimpse of the superstar he would become.

Sanders was a busy young man in 1989. He started careers in both pro baseball and football. And the big life changes didn't stop there. In 1989, he married Carolyn Chambers. The pair had two children, Deiondra and Deion Jr. Sanders also made good on the promise he'd made to his mother years before. He bought her a new house.

Sanders spent the first five years of his football career with the Falcons. He was thriving. But his baseball career was not. The Yankees released him in 1990. They didn't think Sanders could play both sports at a high level, and it was clear that football was his top priority.

Sanders and Carolyn Chambers attend an event in 1995 with Deiondra (*far left*) and Deion Jr (*far right*).

Double-Dipping

On October 11, 1992, Sanders truly was a two-sport star. That afternoon he was on the football field in Miami, Florida, as the Falcons took on the Dolphins. After the game, he flew to Pittsburgh, Pennsylvania, to join the Braves for an evening playoff game against the Pirates. Braves manager Bobby Cox did his best to work with Sanders's intense schedule. "There's never been a problem like this," Cox said. "There's never been a Deion Sanders, either."

Sanders wasn't ready to give up on baseball, though. In 1991, he signed with the Atlanta Braves. The Braves went to the World Series that year, but Sanders could only watch. His NFL contract didn't allow him to play baseball during football season. Sanders didn't want that to happen again, so the Falcons reworked his contract, allowing him to take part in MLB postseason games even during football season.

Sanders kept improving. The 1992 season was his best yet. He batted .304 and stole 26 bases for the Braves. They returned to the World Series. This time, Sanders was there with his team. And he came up big. Sanders batted an amazing .533 in the series and stole five bases. It wasn't enough, though. The Toronto Blue Jays won the series, four games to two.

Sanders runs around the bases during the 1992 World Series.

ON THE MOVE

Sanders developed both his baseball and football careers in Atlanta. But it wasn't long before he was on the move. The Braves traded him to the Cincinnati Reds in 1994. Sanders spent two seasons there as a part-time player. During the 1995 season, the Reds traded him to the San Francisco Giants.

Sanders was also making big changes on the football field. In 1994 he signed with the San Francisco 49ers. He spent only one season with the team, but it was the best of his career. Sanders had six interceptions and returned three of them for touchdowns. He was named the NFL Defensive Player of the Year. He also finished third in league Most Valuable Player voting—an award that almost always goes to an offensive player.

The 49ers went 13–3 during the 1994 regular season. They rolled over the Chicago Bears in their first playoff game. Then they faced the powerful Dallas Cowboys in the National Football Conference Championship. The 49ers were clinging to a late lead as the Cowboys drove the ball. Dallas quarterback Troy Aikman took a snap and dropped back to pass. Sanders was covering Michael Irvin, one of the best receivers in the game. Sanders slipped on the turf. It looked like Irving would be wide open. But Sanders recovered and streaked toward Irving. He knocked the ball away in a huge play that helped seal the win for San Francisco.

The win sent the 49ers to the Super Bowl. That made Sanders the first person in history to play in both a World Series and a Super Bowl. As usual, Sanders came up big when the spotlight was on him. His interception in the fourth quarter helped San Francisco finish off the Los Angeles Chargers. Sanders and the 49ers were Super Bowl champions.

Despite a hugely successful season, Sanders did not re-sign with the 49ers. He was looking for a big payday.

Sanders (*bottom*) runs with the ball during the 1995 Super Bowl.

The "Deion Sanders sweepstakes," as reporters called his search for a new team, dragged through the summer and into the start of the 1995 season. Finally, on September 9, Sanders got the offer he wanted. He signed a seven-year, $35 million contract with the Dallas Cowboys.

The spotlight seemed to follow Sanders. Even though he missed part of the season due to an injury, he helped Dallas to a 12–4 regular season. They cruised through the conference playoffs. For the second season in a row,

Sanders was playing in the biggest game of the year, this time against the Pittsburgh Steelers.

Sanders made a big play in the first quarter of the game. But it wasn't on defense, and it wasn't on a punt return. Sanders came out with the offense and lined up as a wide receiver. He streaked down the right sideline. Aikman heaved a long pass. Sanders cut in front of a defender to snatch the ball for a 47-yard gain. The big play led to a touchdown and helped Dallas take control of the game. The Cowboys won, 27–17. For the second straight season, Sanders was a Super Bowl champion.

Crossover Star

Sanders wanted to be more than just an athlete. In 1994 he released a rap album titled *Prime Time*. In 1995 he hosted the comedy show *Saturday Night Live*. Sanders took part in several sketches and performed two of his songs on the show.

LATE CAREER

Sanders didn't play in MLB at all in 1996. But he returned to the Reds in 1997. He played in 115 games that season, the most in his career. He batted .273 and was second in the National League with 56 stolen bases. It was a good year, but Sanders stepped away from the game when football season came around, and he didn't return to MLB for four years.

Sanders continued to be one of the best cornerbacks in the NFL. He remained with Dallas for five productive seasons. Sanders made the Pro Bowl every year but 1995 when his season was cut short by an injury.

Sanders and his wife, Pilar, attend an event in 2008.

Meanwhile, Sanders's family life was changing. He and Chambers divorced in 1998. A year later, Sanders married actress Pilar Biggers. The pair had two sons, Shilo and Shedeur, and a daughter, Shelomi.

In 2000 the Cowboys released Sanders in an effort to save money. At 33, he was already older than most NFL cornerbacks. He didn't quite have the speed that made him so good in his younger years. But he was still a solid defender and a big star. He signed a seven-year, $56 million contract with Washington. It was a huge commitment for an aging star.

Sanders had a solid first season with Washington. But he wasn't happy with the team. So just before he was supposed to report to training camp in 2001, Sanders surprised the football world by retiring. The move came only a few months after a poor performance in a return to the major leagues with the Reds. After years of being a two-sport star, Sanders was suddenly out of both.

It wasn't the end of his playing career, however. In 2004 Baltimore Ravens defenders Ray Lewis and Corey Fuller convinced Sanders to come out of retirement. The Ravens had one of the best defenses in the league, and Sanders could be a role player. He wouldn't play all the time, but he could enter the game when his skills would be most effective. Sanders chose to wear jersey number 37—his age at the time.

"I think I have unfinished business, particularly on behalf of last season," Sanders said. "The only problem is how can I perform, how long can I stay on the field? That's something I need your prayers about. If I stay on the field, I'm going to make plays."

Sanders had a few highlights left in him. In a 2004 game against the Buffalo Bills, Sanders tracked down a tipped ball for an interception. He ran down the field for a 48-yard touchdown. It was the ninth interception return for a touchdown in his career. At the time, that interception tied him for second on the NFL's all-time list.

In 2005 Sanders played in all 16 games for Baltimore. But it was a disappointing season for the team, and they failed to make the playoffs. In January 2006 Sanders retired from playing again. This time it was for good.

Sanders attends a basketball game with kids Deion Jr (*far left*), Shilo (*center*), and Deiondra (*far right*) in 2003.

FATHER AND COACH

With his career as a professional athlete over, Sanders turned his attention to a broadcasting career. He spent time as a football analyst for CBS's pregame show. He also made appearances on a wide range of other football-related shows. He even served as the host of a Miss USA pageant.

Sanders also focused on family. He spent time with his wife and five kids. In 2008 the family took part in a reality TV show called *Deion & Pilar: Prime Time Love.* The show followed the family's life in small-town Texas.

It featured Sanders's struggles to balance his broadcasting career, marriage, and fatherhood.

In 2011 Sanders was voted into the Pro Football Hall of Fame. "This game means so much to me," he said in his enshrinement speech. "It taught me how to get up, it taught me how to live and play with pain, this game. This game taught me so much about people. It taught me so much about timing. It taught me so much about focus, dedication, submitting one's self, and sacrifices."

Sanders poses with a bust of himself after his enshrinement in the Pro Football Hall of Fame in 2011.

A year later, Sanders started down a new path. He took a coaching job at Prime Prep Academy, a charter school in Texas that he had helped found. He coached there for two years before he was forced to leave after he had a physical confrontation with a school administrator. After that, he spent two years coaching at Triple A Academy in Dallas, Texas.

Sanders passed his love of sports down to his children. In 2017 his youngest sons, Shilo and Shedeur, were playing high school football at Trinity Christian High School in Cedar Hill, Texas. Sanders left Triple A Academy to take a job as the team's offensive coordinator. He was thrilled to have the chance to coach his sons, both of whom were showing great potential on the field.

Shilo followed his father's example, starring as a defensive back. The best high school football players in the US are five-star prospects. In his senior year, Shilo was a four-star prospect. That made him a prized recruit. He had offers from 15 colleges. He chose to take his talents to the University of South Carolina.

Meanwhile, Shedeur was starring as Trinity Christian's quarterback. In his senior season, ESPN ranked him the 12th-best quarterback recruit in the country. He had his choice of colleges. The top programs in the nation wanted him. He got scholarship offers from Alabama, Louisiana State, Florida, and more.

With Shedeur graduating high school in 2020, it was time for Deion Sanders to make another move. The Jackson State University football team offered him a head coaching position. Jackson State didn't play against the top college teams in the US. They competed one step below the highest level. But it was still a huge step for someone who had never coached above the high school level. Sanders was ready for the challenge, and he had a couple of aces up his sleeve. Shedeur committed to Jackson State to play for his dad. "Dad, I got your back," Shedeur wrote on Twitter (now X) when he made the decision. Shilo soon joined them after transferring from South Carolina. The three were ready to take on the world of college football together.

Sanders coaches during a Jackson State game in 2022.

Sanders talks to son Shilo during the 2022 Celebration Bowl.

JACKSON STATE

Coaching his sons in college was a dream come true for Sanders. "It's been wonderful, I've coached my kids their entire life, so it's not new to us," he said. "When we're between the lines I'm Coach Prime. Outside of that I'm Dad. They don't mix the two."

The 2020 football season was unusual. The COVID-19 pandemic forced many schools to cancel or postpone their seasons. It was February 21, 2021, before Sanders made his coaching debut. And it was a success. The Jackson

State Tigers crushed Edward Waters University 53–0. Sanders and his team followed that up with wins over Grambling State University and Mississippi Valley State University. But their winning streak ended there. The Tigers lost their next three games to even their record at 3–3. The team technically finished the season 4–3 after Alcorn State University forfeited the final game because of the pandemic.

The college football schedule had largely returned to normal by the fall of 2021. Expectations were high for Sanders and the Tigers. Sanders had already proved himself a strong recruiter. He was bringing some of the best players in the nation to Jackson State. The team looked primed for success.

Shilo Sanders plays for Jackson State in a 2021 game.

The Tigers beat Florida A&M University in their season opener, 7–6. The tight defensive battle was not a sign of things to come, however. In the second game, Shedeur threw three touchdown passes as the Tigers beat Tennessee State University 38–16.

On December 4, 2021, Sanders led the Tigers into the Southwestern Athletic Conference (SWAC) Championship Game. They faced the Prairie View A&M University Panthers. Prairie View took an early lead. But Jackson State used a second-half surge to put the game out of reach. The win improved their season record to 11–1 and sent them to the Celebration Bowl in Atlanta, Georgia, to face the South Carolina State Bulldogs.

The game started out well for the Tigers. Shedeur threw a 7-yard touchdown pass in the first quarter to give them a 7–0 lead. But then things took a turn for the worse. The Bulldogs dominated the rest of the game, sending Sanders home with a 31–10 loss.

"South Carolina State kicked our butts," Sanders said after the game. "Every way, every fashion. Outphysicaled us. Out threw us. Much more disciplined than us. And I feel like we were overconfident, and overlooked them as if they were just going to hand us the game."

The 2022 season played out similar to the previous season. Sanders had a roster loaded with talent, and the Tigers rolled over every team they faced. They went 11–0 in the regular season. Then they won the SWAC Championship Game again, beating the Southern University Jaguars 43–24.

That set up a return to the Celebration Bowl to face the North Carolina Central Eagles in Sanders's final game as Jackson State's head coach. The Tigers needed one more win to complete a perfect season. The game was a classic. The Eagles jumped out to a 10–0 lead, but the Tigers came back. In the final seconds of the fourth quarter, Jackson State trailed by seven points. Shedeur hit receiver Travis Hunter with a touchdown pass on the final play to force overtime. But the dream of a perfect season died there. The Eagles scored on their overtime possession, while Shedeur's last desperation pass fell incomplete. The Eagles won, 41–34.

It was a disappointing finish for Sanders. But already, he was looking ahead to bigger things.

Shedeur Sanders looks to pass in the 2022 Celebration Bowl.

Health Troubles

Sanders struggled with his health in 2021. After surgery on a dislocated toe, he developed blood clots in his legs. His left leg swelled up. It was a serious condition. Doctors feared that they would have to amputate his lower left leg. They ended up taking off only two of his toes.

WELCOME TO COLORADO

On December 3, 2022, two weeks before the Celebration Bowl, the University of Colorado Boulder hired Sanders to be its next head coach. It was a surprising move. Sanders had enjoyed success with Jackson State. But Colorado was a Pacific-12 Conference school, which put them at the highest level of college football. Sanders had gained a reputation as a great recruiter. But some wondered if he was ready to take over such a high-profile program.

"There were a number of highly qualified and impressive candidates interested in becoming the next head football coach at Colorado, but none of them had the pedigree, the knowledge and the ability to connect with student-athletes like Deion Sanders," said Colorado athletic director Rick George.

Sanders had his work cut out for him. From 2006 to 2022, Colorado had only two winning seasons. But Sanders was up for the challenge.

Sanders speaks to press at the
University of Colorado Boulder in 2022.

Traditionally, a new head coach takes on the roster left behind by the previous coach. Athletes sign on for four years with a college. Most new coaches honor that commitment and slowly tailor the roster to their needs over a few years.

Sanders made waves in the college football world when he made it clear that he wouldn't follow that route. He wanted his own roster right away. Sanders told most of Colorado's existing players that he didn't have a place for them. He wanted to free up space for transfers—including ten players that followed him from Jackson State (both of his younger sons among them).

"I'm coming, and when I get here, it's gonna be change," Sanders announced to the team. "So, I want you all to get ready to go ahead and jump in the [transfer] portal. . . . We're bringing kids that are smart, tough, fast, disciplined with character. That's the ones we're gonna get. Is that you?"

Sanders talks to son Shilo before a game in October 2023.

It may not have been a popular decision. But Sanders knew that he had a limited opportunity to turn around a team that had gone 1-11 the season before. The real question was, would it work?

All eyes were on Sanders and the Buffaloes when they opened the 2023 season on the road against TCU. Their big upset of the Horned Frogs sent shock waves through the college football world. Sanders was defiant in victory.

Sanders coaches from the sidelines during an October 2023 game.

He wanted his doubters to know that he was ready to succeed.

Heading into the second game, the Buffaloes were ranked number 22 in the nation. They backed it up, beating Nebraska 36–14. Next, they took down in-state rival Colorado State 43–35. It was looking like Sanders had delivered sooner than anyone could have expected.

But it wouldn't be that easy. Tougher times were on the way.

UNCERTAIN FUTURE

Colorado's hot start didn't last. They lost their next two games to Oregon and the University of Southern California—two teams ranked in the top 10. They managed a conference win over Arizona State to move to 4–2 on the season. But it was all downhill from there. The team lost its last six games. The low point came on November 17, 2023, when unranked Washington State University destroyed the Buffaloes 56–14. Shedeur missed the end of the season with a broken back, and his once high NFL draft stock had taken a big fall.

It was a difficult time for Sanders. Many of his players were leaving the program. Highly prized recruits who had committed to Colorado were backing out. Sanders was frustrated. He made a comment about players having too much freedom. He said that they shouldn't be able to visit other schools after committing to a college.

Sportsperson of the Year

In November of 2023, *Sports Illustrated* named Sanders its Sportsperson of the Year. The award honors the "athlete or team whose performance that year most embodies the spirit of sportsmanship and achievement." The magazine's staff credited Sanders with reviving Colorado's football program and adding a new level of excitement to the school's campus and community.

Sanders accepts the Sportsperson of the Year award in 2023.

The comments did not sit well with his recruits. Soon after, several more recruits backed out of their commitments. Sanders had hoped for a quick rebuild at Colorado. It was starting to look like success might be

a much longer process than he'd hoped.

Throughout his career, Sanders has embraced challenge. Few athletes would have attempted to juggle NFL and MLB careers. And fewer still would have succeeded at both. Sanders has climbed the ranks of college coaching. In only four years, he went from a high school coordinator to the head coach of one of the highest profile college football programs in the country. How will he face these new challenges? His fans can't wait to find out.

Sanders during a game in October 2023

IMPORTANT DATES

1967   Deion Luwynn Sanders is born on August 9 in Fort Myers, Florida.

1985   Sanders graduates from North Fort Myers High School.

He accepts a scholarship to play football for Florida State University.

1988   Sanders signs a contract with the New York Yankees.

1989   The Atlanta Falcons select Sanders with the fifth pick in the NFL draft.

He makes his debut for both the Yankees and the Falcons.

1991   Sanders signs with the Atlanta Braves.

1992   Sanders bats .533 in the World Series with the Braves, but they lose to the Toronto Blue Jays, four games to two.

1995   Sanders wins a Super Bowl with the San Francisco 49ers, becoming the first athlete ever to compete in both a World Series and a Super Bowl.

1996   Sanders wins a second Super Bowl, this time with the Dallas Cowboys.

1997   Sanders has his best MLB season, batting .273 with 56 stolen bases for the Cincinnati Reds.

2000   The Cowboys release Sanders. He signs with Washington.

2001   Sanders retires from both baseball and football.

2004   Sanders comes out of retirement to play for the Baltimore Ravens.

2006   Sanders retires from the NFL, this time for good.

2011   Sanders is enshrined in the Pro Football Hall of Fame.

2012   Sanders becomes head coach for Prime Prep Academy.

2017   Sanders joins the coaching staff at Trinity Christian High School so he can coach his sons Shedeur and Shilo.

2020   Jackson State hires Sanders as its head coach. Shedeur and Shilo join their father on the team.

2022   The University of Colorado hires Sanders to be head coach.

2023   After a hot start, Colorado struggles to a 4–8 record.

SOURCE NOTES

9   Derek Peterson, "Everything Deion Sanders said after Colorado's upset win over TCU," *Saturday Out West*, September 2, 2023, https://saturdayoutwest.com/colorado-buffaloes/everything -deion-sanders-said-after-colorados-upset-win-over-tcu/.

10 Steve Rushin, "Catch-21 The nomadic Deion Sanders longs to be seen as just a hardworking athlete, but he can't escape his own hype," *Sports Illustrated*, July 31, 1995, https://vault.si.com /vault/1995/07/31/catch-21-the-nomadic-deion-sanders-longs -to-be-seen-as-just-a-hardworking-athlete-but-he-cant-escape -his-own-hype.

13 Jim Henry, "Prime Time Rewind: Bowden talks Sanders," *Tallahassee Democrat*, August 1, 2015, https://www.tallahassee .com/story/sports/college/fsu/football/2015/08/01/prime-time -rewind-bowden-talks-sanders/31007101/.

15 Craig Barnes, "Yankees vets tell Sanders: You've got wrong number," *Sun Sentinel*, February 26, 1989, https://web.archive. org/web/20210630140358/https://www.sun-sentinel.com/news/ fl-xpm-1989-02-26-8901110363-story.html.

17 Kevin Borba, "Looking back at Deion Sanders' iconic NFL Draft quotes," *Athlon Sports*, April 27, 2023, https://athlonsports.com /college-football/looking-back-at-deion-sanders-iconic-nfl-draft -quotes.

20 Edward Sutelan, "How Deion Sanders played baseball and football on the same day: Revisiting his historic 1992 NFL, MLB attempt," *The Sporting News*, October 11, 2023, https://www .sportingnews.com/us/mlb/news/how-deion-sanders-played -baseball-and-football-same-day-revisiting-his-historic-1992 -nfl-mlb-attempt/afb44244f3f6e7ee364640f5.

23 Timothy W. Smith, "PRO FOOTBALL; Fight for Sanders Revs Up a Notch," *The New York Times*, August 27, 1995, https://www .nytimes.com/1995/08/27/sports/pro-football-fight-for-sanders -revs-up-a-notch.html.

26 Camille Powell, "Sanders Returns to Ravens for Some Unfinished Business," *The Washington Post*, June 9, 2005, https://www .washingtonpost.com/archive/sports/2005/06/09/sanders-returns -to-ravens-for-some-unfinished-business/5347d522-9d65-4bb4 -a8c2-9f4234725407/.

28 Brian Schaible, "Looking back at Deion Sanders 2011 Hall of Fame Speech," SI.com, August 2, 2023, https://www.si.com /college/colorado/buffs-social/looking-back-at-deion-sanders -2011-hall-of-fame-speech.

30 Michelle Kaufman, "Deion Sanders' quarterback son to debut vs. FAMU in Orange Blossom Classic on Sunday," *Miami Herald*, September 4, 2021, https://www.miamiherald.com/sports /article253897578.html.

31 Kaufman.

33 Khari Thompson, "Don't let Jackson State football's ugly Celebration Bowl loss overshadow historic season," *Mississippi Clarion Ledger*, December 19, 2021, https://www.clarionledger .com/story/sports/college/jackson-state/2021/12/18/jackson -state-football-score-clebration-bowl-south-carolina-state /6468077001/.

35 Pete Thamel, "Colorado Buffaloes name Deion Sanders as head coach," ESPN.com, December 3, 2022, https://www.espn.com /college-football/story/_/id/35176614/colorado-buffaloes-name -deion-sanders-head-coach.

37 Julia Stumbaugh, "Deion Sanders Given Support from Colorado AD After 57 Players Enter Transfer Portal," *Bleacher Report*, May 4, 2023, https://bleacherreport.com/articles/10075009-deion -sanders-given-support-from-colorado-ad-after-57-players -enter-transfer-portal.

40 Chris Chavez, "Sports Illustrated's Sportsperson Of The Year: By The Numbers," *Sports Illustrated*, December 1, 2017, https:// www.si.com/sportsperson/2017/12/01/sportsperson-of-the-year -numbers-notes.

SELECTED BIBLIOGRAPHY

"Football Stats and History." Pro Football Reference. https://www.pro
-football-reference.com.

Ramsey, Donovan X. "Deion Sanders Enters His Prime." *GQ Sports*,
January 9, 2023. https://www.gq.com/story/deion-sanders-style-hall
-of-fame-february-cover.

Rushin, Steve. "Catch-21 The Nomadic Deion Sanders Longs to be Seen
as Just a Hardworking Athlete, but He Can't Escape His Own Hype."
Sports Illustrated, July 31, 1995. https://vault.si.com/vault/1995
/07/31/catch-21-the-nomadic-deion-sanders-longs-to-be-seen-as
-just-a-hardworking-athlete-but-he-cant-escape-his-own-hype.

Sutelan, Edward. "How Deion Sanders played baseball and football on
the same day: Revisiting his historic 1992 NFL, MLB attempt." *The
Sporting News*, October 11, 2023. https://www.sportingnews.com/us
/mlb/news/how-deion-sanders-played-baseball-and-football-same
-day-revisiting-his-historic-1992-nfl-mlb-attempt
/afb44244f3f6e7ee364640f5.

Taylor, Jean-Jacques. *Coach Prime: Deion Sanders and the Making of
Men*. New York: Mariner Books, 2023.

LEARN MORE

Hill, Christina. *Inside the Dallas Cowboys*. Minneapolis: Lerner
    Publications, 2023.

Pro Football Hall of Fame–Deion Sanders
    https://www.profootballhof.com/players/deion-sanders/

Pro Football Reference–Deion Sanders
    https://www.pro-football-reference.com/players/S/SandDe00.htm

Stewart, Audrey. *G.O.A.T. Football Cornerbacks*. Minneapolis: Lerner
    Publications, 2025.

University of Colorado Athletics–Football
    https://cubuffs.com/sports/football

Weber, Margaret. *Florida State Seminoles*. New York: AV2 by Weigl,
    2020.

INDEX

PHOTO ACKNOWLEDGMENTS

Image credits: AP Photo/Ryan Kang, p. 2; AP Photo/LM Otero, p. 6; Ron Jenkins/Stringer/Getty Images, p. 8; John Coletti/Getty Images, p. 10; AP Photo/Steve Nesius, p. 11; Focus On Sport/Getty Images, pp. 13, 18; AP Photo/Ron Frehm, p. 14; AP Photo, p. 16; AP Photo/David Banks, p. 17; AP Photo/Ron Heflin, p. 19; V.J. Lovero/Getty Images, p. 21; AP Photo/Kevin Terrell, p. 23, 38; Michael Loccisano/Getty Images, p. 25; Ray Amati/Stringer/Getty Images, p. 27; Zuma Press, Inc./Alamy, p. 28; AP Photo/Rogelio V. Solis, p. 30; AP Photo/Jason Getz/Atlanta Journal-Constitution, p. 31; AP Photo/Matthew Hinton, p. 32; AP Photo/Nick Tre. Smith/Icon Sportswire, p. 34; AP Photo/David Zalubowski, p. 36; AP Photo/David Dennis/Icon Sportswire, p. 37; Tom Cooper/Stringer/Getty Images, p. 40; AP Photo/Ross D. Franklin, p. 41.

Cover: AP Photo/Nick Tre. Smith/Icon Sportswire.